REUSABLE ROCKETS

by Gregory L. Vogt

www.focusreaders.com

Copyright © 2023 by Focus Readers®, Mendota Heights, MN 55120. All rights reserved. No part of this book may be reproduced or utilized in any form or by any means without written permission from the publisher.

Focus Readers is distributed by North Star Editions:
sales@northstareditions.com | 888-417-0195

Produced for Focus Readers by Red Line Editorial.

Content Consultant: Matthew Pryal, PhD, Assistant Professor of Astronomy, University of Virginia

Photographs ©: Tony Gray and Tim Powers/NASA, cover, 1; Tony Gutierrez/AP Images, 4–5, 28–29; NASA, 7, 16–17, 20, 38–39; Bill Ingalls/NASA, 9, 41; Blue Origin/NASA Flight Opportunities, 10–11; Red Line Editorial, 12; Jim Grossmann/NASA, 14; George Shelton/NASA, 18; Kim Shiflett/NASA, 22–23, 24; SpaceX, 27; Blue Origin/NASA, 31; Shutterstock Images, 33; Matt Hartman/AP Images, 34–35; Ken Ulbrich/NASA, 37; Reginald Mathalone/NurPhoto/AP Images, 43; Dimitri Gerondidakis/NASA, 45

Library of Congress Cataloging-in-Publication Data
Library of Congress Cataloging-in-Publication Data is available on the Library of Congress website.

ISBN
979-8-88998-000-1 (hardcover)
979-8-88998-001-8 (paperback)
979-8-88998-003-2 (ebook pdf)
979-8-88998-002-5 (hosted ebook)

Printed in the United States of America
Mankato, MN
May, 2023

ABOUT THE AUTHOR

Gregory L. Vogt is an assistant professor at the Baylor College of Medicine in Houston, Texas. He is a former classroom teacher, science museum director, and educational specialist in the NASA Astronaut Office. He has authored more than 100 books. Occasionally, Vogt presents science and magic shows to children.

TABLE OF CONTENTS

CHAPTER 1
Blasting Off 5

CHAPTER 2
It's Rocket Science 11

CHAPTER 3
Trial and Error 17

CHAPTER 4
Early SpaceX Work 23

FOCUS ON TECHNOLOGY
Landing a Rocket 26

CHAPTER 5
Blue Origin 29

CHAPTER 6
Multiple Methods 35

CHAPTER 7
Many Missions 39

PERSON OF IMPACT
Elon Musk 44

Focus on Reusable Rockets • 46
Glossary • 47
To Learn More • 48
Index • 48

CHAPTER 1

BLASTING OFF

Imagine boarding a **capsule** at the top of a tall rocket. You and five other space tourists strap yourselves in to a reclined seat that faces upward. The countdown reaches zero, and the rocket engines fire, launching the spacecraft. A few minutes after liftoff, the capsule separates from the rocket. As the rocket heads back to the launch site, the capsule coasts upward. Large windows give spectacular views of the blue curve of Earth.

By August 2022, Blue Origin had used its New Shepard rocket to make six flights bringing people to space.

Then the capsule begins falling back to Earth. It plows into the **atmosphere**. Next its parachutes open. Just above the ground, thruster rockets slow the capsule for a soft landing. You leave the capsule, and workers prepare it for the next flight. The capsule is mounted on top of a rocket again. This rocket is refueled. Later, it will take more people to space.

People have used rockets for hundreds of years. Chinese fireworks began using rockets in the 1200s CE. Large arrows were attached to tubes filled with gunpowder. When the rocket was ignited, the arrow flew a long distance.

In the 1950s, scientists and engineers worked to launch **satellites** into space. One of these engineers was Wernher von Braun. Von Braun was the main designer of the Saturn V rocket. This rocket launched astronauts to the moon. But each

⚠ Dr. Wernher von Braun stands in front of the Saturn V launch vehicle's engines.

Saturn V rocket could be used only one time. Von Braun wanted to build rockets that could travel to and from space many times. He designed a giant rocket with a winged spacecraft on top.

Von Braun's design had three main parts called **stages**. The stages would stack on top of one another. The first stage would be a huge rocket with 51 engines. When this rocket ran out of fuel, it would fall back to Earth. Parachutes would bring it back safely so it could be used again.

After the rocket's first stage detached, the second stage would ignite. This stage would also parachute back and be reused. The third stage would be a winged spacecraft. It would **orbit** Earth before flying home to a runway.

However, Von Braun's reusable rocket was never built. It was too complicated and expensive. At the time, engineers were only beginning to learn how to build space rockets. Many rockets crashed or exploded right after liftoff. Each failure meant going back to the drawing board to try again.

▲ By 2023, SpaceX had launched more than 190 reusable rockets.

Reusable rockets took years of hard work to develop. But new materials and technologies have become available. A few private companies have begun to build and launch reusable rockets.

CHAPTER 2

IT'S ROCKET SCIENCE

Rocket science is all about thrust. Thrust is a pushing force that propels the rocket forward. **Propellants** are pumped to the rocket's engines, where they are burned. This process creates hot gases. These gases are channeled so they are released in just one direction. When the gases leave the rocket's engine, thrust is created. When enough thrust is produced, the rocket lifts off the ground.

Blue Origin's New Shepard rocket is designed for a vertical landing.

As the gas shoots out of the engine, the rocket moves in the opposite direction. Engines that shoot out more gas will produce more thrust. Increasing the gas's speed will also produce more thrust. More thrust makes the rocket move faster.

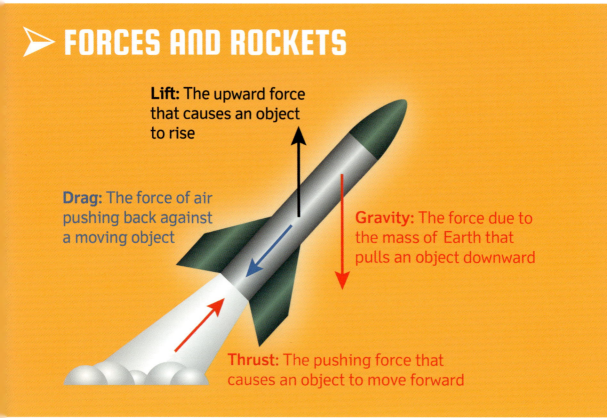

FORCES AND ROCKETS

Lift: The upward force that causes an object to rise

Drag: The force of air pushing back against a moving object

Gravity: The force due to the mass of Earth that pulls an object downward

Thrust: The pushing force that causes an object to move forward

Engineers try to design a rocket's body to be as light as possible. That's because heavier rockets require more force to move. To produce more force, rockets need more propellants. However, some propellants, such as hydrogen and oxygen, must be kept in separate tanks. That makes the rocket heavier. Burning propellants also creates a lot of heat, so engines need a cooling system.

Rockets also need a steering system. A simple steering system uses fins. These small wings stick out from the rocket's side. The fins act like the feathers on an arrow that keep it flying straight. If the rocket goes off course, the fins can tilt. Air will hit the tilted fins and push the rocket back to the right path. Other steering systems use engines that tilt. If the rocket goes off course, the engines tilt the other way. The angled thrust pushes the rocket back on course.

▲ An Atlas V rocket's fairing closes around its payload, NASA's Mars Science Laboratory.

Rockets may have a **payload** carrier as well. Payloads can be anything from satellites that orbit Earth to spacecraft that travel to other planets. A shell called a fairing covers the payload for launch. Once the rocket is in space, the shell opens to release the payload.

Landing a rocket is difficult. For instance, suppose a rocket is flying back to a landing zone. First, the rocket's engines must restart to slow the rocket's fall. Just above the ground, the speed must reach zero, or else the rocket will crash. Then, landing feet must extend as the rocket touches down.

THINK ABOUT IT

A reusable rocket must be able to take off and land. Why would making a rocket reusable double the engineering challenges?

CHAPTER 3

TRIAL AND ERROR

The first partially reusable rocket was the space shuttle. The National Aeronautics and Space Administration (NASA) flew the first shuttle in 1981. The shuttle was made up of four parts. A winged spaceship called an orbiter carried astronauts and payloads. The orbiter attached to the side of a huge propellant tank. Two **booster** rockets also attached to the tank. During liftoff, the boosters quickly used up their fuel. Then

Space shuttles often carried people and supplies to the International Space Station.

⚠ A ship pulls a rocket booster from the space shuttle *Discovery* back to shore.

they fell from the shuttle and parachuted into the ocean. They floated until ships found them and towed them back to land to be reused.

Minutes later, the propellant tank also dropped off the rocket. Unlike the boosters, it would not be used again. Instead, **friction** with the air caused the tank to burn up as it fell back toward Earth.

Next, the orbiter used small engines on its tail to rocket into orbit. When the shuttle's mission was over, astronauts flew the orbiter back to Earth. There, it landed on a runway. Then the orbiter could be reused for more space missions.

Making parts of the shuttle reusable was supposed to save money on space launches. But creating the space shuttle was complicated. Safely leaving Earth's atmosphere is difficult. So is reentering. Sometimes, shuttle parts failed. Two shuttles exploded, and astronauts died.

In 1996, NASA tried to develop a fully reusable rocket. It was called the X-33. The X-33 was designed to be launched upright. No parts would fall off on the way to outer space. Instead, the entire rocket would return from space and land on a runway. Tail fins and small wings would allow the X-33 to fly like an airplane on its return.

NASA engineers began testing this design. But they had problems creating the propellant tanks.

⚠ This artist's illustration shows a design for the X-33.

The tanks needed to hold massive amounts of propellant. But they also needed to be very light. Engineers could not figure out how to make the tanks do this. Plans for the X-33 rocket were canceled a few years later.

In 2004, President George W. Bush announced that NASA would phase out the space shuttle program in a few years. NASA would keep using the space shuttles to finish building the International Space Station (ISS). But after that, NASA would focus on missions to deep space. Canceling the space shuttles would allow NASA to devote more time and money to this goal.

However, canceling the shuttles would create a problem. US astronauts would still need a way to travel to and from the ISS. By the time the ISS was completed in 2011, private companies were already hard at work designing and testing reusable rockets. The companies hoped to take over sending astronauts and supplies to the ISS.

THINK ABOUT IT

Why do you think NASA canceled the space shuttle program if astronauts still needed to travel to and from the ISS?

CHAPTER 4

EARLY SPACEX WORK

A company called SpaceX began building reusable rockets in the 2000s. Its first rocket was called the Falcon 1. It had one engine. Later, SpaceX began making the Falcon 9. This rocket's first stage had nine engines. A spacecraft called Dragon sat at the rocket's top. It could parachute into the ocean after its mission and be reused.

At first, each Falcon 9 rocket was used only once. But after several successful flights, SpaceX was

The bell-shaped Dragon capsule can attach to a Falcon 9 rocket to carry cargo to space.

➤ THE FALCON 9 ROCKET

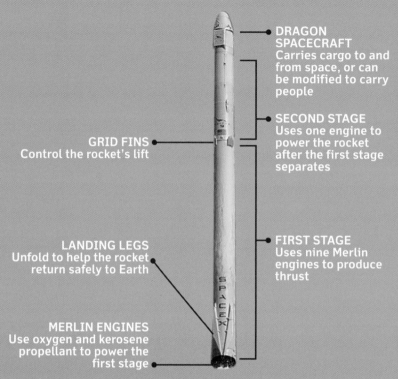

DRAGON SPACECRAFT
Carries cargo to and from space, or can be modified to carry people

SECOND STAGE
Uses one engine to power the rocket after the first stage separates

GRID FINS
Control the rocket's lift

FIRST STAGE
Uses nine Merlin engines to produce thrust

LANDING LEGS
Unfold to help the rocket return safely to Earth

MERLIN ENGINES
Use oxygen and kerosene propellant to power the first stage

ready to try landing and recovering the first stage. To practice this difficult task, SpaceX built a rocket called Grasshopper. Grasshopper was a Falcon 9 first stage with only one engine. It had four legs for landing. Grasshopper never went to space. But SpaceX engineers used it to conduct many tests.

Finally, they were ready to try landing a Falcon 9 first stage. Their first attempt took place in January 2015. Minutes after launch, the first stage separated from the rocket. As the upper stage continued on toward space, the first stage fell back to Earth. Gas jets and small wings, or fins, helped steer the first stage toward a floating barge in the ocean. One minute before touchdown, the rocket's fin control system failed. The test ended in a crash.

But engineers kept working. They attempted another landing in April. This one failed, too. But in December, a Falcon 9 first stage safely touched down on a landing pad. In April 2016, a Falcon 9 first stage landed on a ship after launching a payload. And in March 2017, the first relaunch of a Falcon 9 took place. SpaceX was officially in the reusable rocket business.

FOCUS ON TECHNOLOGY

LANDING A ROCKET

In 2017, SpaceX brought several Falcon 9 first stages safely back from space. One of these landings took place on May 1. Approximately two and a half minutes after launching, the first stage's nine engines shut down. Next, the rocket stages separated. As the second stage headed into space, the first stage changed its direction by firing small nitrogen gas jets. Three of its engines fired to send it back toward the launch site. Then more gas jets turned the first stage around so that its bottom pointed toward the ground. Another engine burn slowed the first stage's fall. To help keep the rocket aimed properly, four small fins opened near the rocket's upper end.

The engines shut down again, and the rocket gained speed as it neared the ground. Thirty seconds before landing, the rocket was falling at a speed of approximately 621 miles per hour

▲ A Falcon 9 rocket lands at the Kennedy Space Center.

(1,000 km/h). Next, it did a final landing burn. This slowed the rocket down. Ten seconds from touchdown, four landing legs opened. Then the rocket touched down on the landing pad.

CHAPTER 5

BLUE ORIGIN

Meanwhile, a company called Blue Origin was working on a different type of reusable rocket. Called New Shepard, this rocket was named after Alan Shepard, the first US astronaut to fly to space. Unlike the SpaceX rockets, which were made to go into orbit, New Shepard was designed to carry tourists to space for just a short time. New Shepard is a one-stage rocket. It is 60 feet (18 m) tall. It has a bell-shaped capsule

On July 20, 2021, New Shepard made its first crewed launch and landing. Four people rode in it.

on top. This capsule has room to hold six people. New Shepard has one liquid-fuel rocket engine at its base. Fins near the rocket's base can tilt to steer the rocket.

Blue Origin began building New Shepard in the 2000s. Throughout the 2010s, the company did many test flights. It reached some milestones before SpaceX. For example, Blue Origin successfully landed a rocket in November 2015. And it relaunched used rockets in 2016.

In 2021, New Shepard made its first launch carrying passengers. Four people rode to and from the edge of space. Since then, New Shepard rockets have brought several sets of tourists to space. A powerful engine launches each rocket up into the air. After slightly more than two minutes, the capsule separates from the booster. For about four minutes, the capsule flies through space. It

⚠ Parachutes help the New Shepard crew capsule make a soft landing when it returns to Earth.

reaches an **altitude** of about 66 miles (106 km). Then, gravity causes it to fall back down to Earth. For part of the flight, passengers feel weightless. They float in the capsule and look out its windows.

Meanwhile, the booster rocket returns to a landing pad near the launch site. The rocket lands vertically on it. It fires its engine a second time to decrease its speed. Fins and drag brakes also help steer and slow the rocket. Then the four legs of its landing gear unfold, and the rocket touches down.

By this time, the capsule has started falling back to Earth, too. First, parachutes open to decrease its speed. Then, three more parachutes open to help it drift slowly down to the ground. Just before the capsule touches down, jets of air shoot from the bottom to cushion the landing.

In the 2010s, Blue Origin began work on a second type of rocket. This one is known as New Glenn. It is named after John Glenn, the first US astronaut to orbit Earth. Unlike New Shepard, New Glenn is designed to reach orbit. The huge rocket stands more than 320 feet (98 m) tall. It is built to carry very large payloads. Its fairing can hold up to 50 tons (45 metric tons).

⚠ New Glenn's fairing is 23 feet (7 m) wide. It's designed to carry satellites and other large payloads.

The New Glenn rocket has two stages. The first stage is designed to be reusable. This stage flies back to Earth. It can land on a ship in the ocean. Later, it can be reused for another flight.

After the rocket's first stage separates, the second stage and fairing fall away, too. Then the payload continues on into space. Blue Origin planned to send payloads to the ISS or even farther. As of early 2023, no New Glenn launches had happened. But Blue Origin had plans to send satellites to space.

CHAPTER 6

MULTIPLE METHODS

Vertical launches are not the only method being used for reusable rockets. For example, a company called Virgin Galactic has a two-part launch system. This system starts on an airport runway. It uses a carrier aircraft to help launch a vehicle called SpaceShipTwo. The carrier is called WhiteKnightTwo. It looks like two airplanes joined together wing to wing. It takes off from a runway. SpaceShipTwo is carried below its center wing.

Virgin Galactic's SpaceShipTwo is designed to carry two pilots and six space tourists.

SpaceShipTwo is released when it is 9.5 miles (15.2 km) above the ground. It fires its rocket engine and climbs to just over 50 miles (80 km). Because SpaceShipTwo starts out high above the ground, it does not need to use as much fuel to climb upward. After a few minutes, it flies back down to land on a runway.

The system faced a few problems in the 2010s, including a crash. But SpaceShipTwo successfully reached space in 2018. And by 2021, it had completed crewed missions. Virgin Galactic also sold tickets for rides on SpaceShipTwo. As of early 2023, commercial flights hadn't started.

In the 2010s, Sierra Nevada Corporation began testing a reusable spacecraft called Dream Chaser. The spacecraft had foldable wings. It launched in a shell on top of a rocket. This shell would open once the rocket reached space. It

Scientists test the Dream Chaser spacecraft at NASA's Dryden Flight Research Center in California.

would release Dream Chaser, which would then use its own engines to travel.

A cargo module called Shooting Star could attach to Dream Chaser. Together, they could hold more than 10,000 pounds (4,500 kg). The module was designed to fall off and burn up during the return journey. Meanwhile, Dream Chaser would glide back to land on a runway. NASA planned to send cargo to the ISS this way in the 2020s.

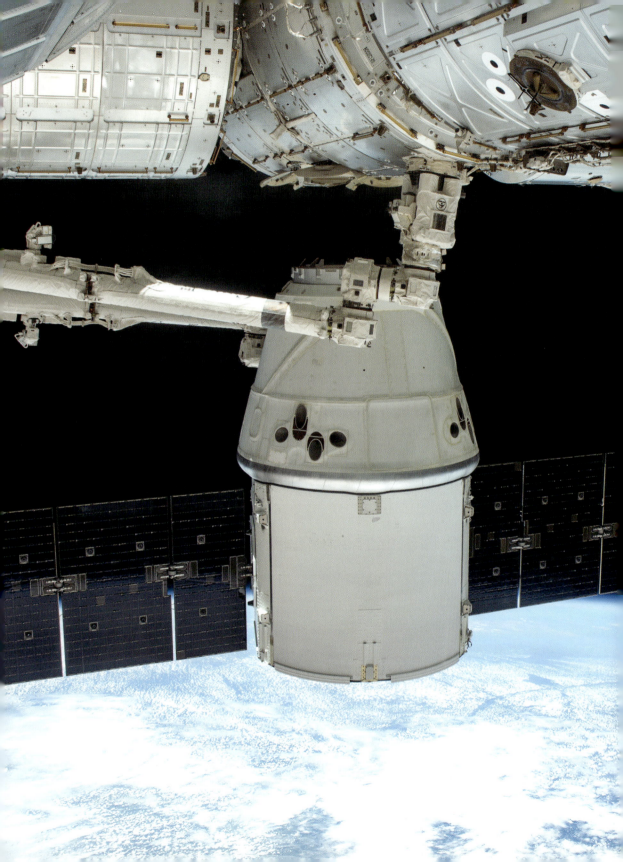

CHAPTER 7

MANY MISSIONS

Reusable rockets are already carrying out many missions. In 2022 alone, SpaceX launched 61 reusable rockets. That was one-third of all rocket launches that year. Most of these missions used the Falcon 9 rocket. Many carried satellites as payloads. Others brought astronauts and supplies to and from the ISS.

For many missions, SpaceX partners with NASA. But SpaceX also makes private flights.

In 2012, Dragon became the first commercial spacecraft to bring supplies to the ISS.

Companies pay SpaceX to carry payloads. And in 2021, SpaceX began bringing civilians to space. Passengers paid $55 million to ride in the Crew Dragon spacecraft.

Work on Crew Dragon had begun back in the 2010s. This version of the Dragon spacecraft has a pressurized section. It provides life support and other things passengers need. Crew Dragon made a test flight to the ISS in March 2019. A dummy rode inside it. Sensors showed what astronauts would experience.

Crew Dragon returned to the ISS in May 2020. This time, it carried passengers. It brought them

> **THINK ABOUT IT**
> What are some advantages of not having crew onboard a spacecraft? What are some disadvantages?

⚠ Dragon's first crewed mission landed safely in the Pacific Ocean on August 2, 2020.

safely back to Earth in August. Two astronauts made this first journey. But Crew Dragon can hold up to seven people. It can also be used to carry delicate cargo back to Earth. Parachutes help it make a soft landing.

SpaceX was also working on Starship. This huge spacecraft was designed to make long journeys and carry huge loads. It has two parts. Together, they stand 394 feet (120 m) tall. The bottom part is a Falcon Super Heavy rocket. It uses about 30 powerful engines to blast off. Then it falls back to Earth, where it lands to be reused.

The top half is a spacecraft that goes into orbit. Reaching space with such a large load uses up lots of fuel. So, SpaceX plans to launch a tanker, too. The tanker would meet up with the spacecraft and refuel it. That way, Starship would have enough fuel to continue its journey. Then the tanker would return to Earth. It could be refilled and used again. Meanwhile, Starship would keep flying further into space.

Starship's huge fairing is 59 feet (18 m) tall and 30 feet (9 m) wide. It can hold large objects, such

⚠ By 2023, SpaceX had built Starship and was getting ready to launch it.

as telescopes. Or it could transport passengers and cargo. Up to 100 people could ride inside.

As of February 2023, Starship had not yet gone into orbit. But SpaceX had plans for a launch. SpaceX and NASA were also working on a version of Starship that would travel to the moon. And one day, rockets might even send people to Mars.

PERSON OF IMPACT

ELON MUSK

Elon Musk is the founder of SpaceX. Musk was born in South Africa in 1971. As a child, he was very interested in computers. He learned how to write computer programs. When he was 12 years old, he created and sold a computer game called *Blaster*.

Musk moved to Canada when he was 17 to attend Queen's University. Three years later, he transferred to the University of Pennsylvania. There, he studied physics and business. Musk then moved to Stanford University in California. Shortly afterward, he created an internet company called Zip2.

Musk sold the company for many millions of dollars. He went on to form several other companies. Some helped develop electric cars and solar power. Musk started SpaceX in 2002. The company focused on building reusable

⚠ Elon Musk reveals the Dragon 2 spacecraft at the SpaceX headquarters.

rockets. Its rockets include the Falcon 9 and Falcon Heavy.

SpaceX's rockets are changing space transportation. Because the rockets can be used many times, they help reduce the cost of flying to space. But Musk's vision goes beyond launching satellites, cargo, and people into orbit. His team is working on missions to the moon. He even hopes to establish a colony on Mars.

FOCUS ON
REUSABLE ROCKETS

Write your answers on a separate piece of paper.

1. What are four advantages of using reusable rockets rather than single-use rockets?

2. If you had the opportunity to become a space tourist, which rocket would you like to ride? Why?

3. Which reusable spacecraft lands in the ocean?
- **A.** New Shepard
- **B.** Dragon
- **C.** SpaceShipTwo

4. What would happen if a rocket's steering fins tilted in the wrong direction?
- **A.** The rocket would go further off course.
- **B.** The rocket's stages would separate too soon.
- **C.** The rocket would use up its fuel too quickly.

Answer key on page 48.

GLOSSARY

altitude
Height above the ground.

atmosphere
The layers of gases that surround a planet or moon.

booster
The first stage of a large rocket, or a small rocket added to the side of a large rocket for extra thrust.

capsule
The section of a spacecraft that carries the crew and often returns to Earth by parachute.

friction
A force generated by the rubbing of one thing against another.

orbit
To repeatedly follow a curved path around another object because of gravity.

payload
An object carried to space by a rocket or other vehicle.

propellants
A combination of fuel and oxygen that burns in a rocket engine to create thrust.

satellites
Objects or vehicles that orbit a planet or moon, often to collect information.

stages
Segments of a larger rocket that drop off after using all of their fuel.

TO LEARN MORE

BOOKS

Hamilton, John. *Humans to Mars*. Minneapolis: Abdo Publishing, 2019.

Moon, Walt K. *Rockets and Space Travel*. San Diego: ReferencePoint Press, 2023.

Radley, Gail. *The Space Encyclopedia*. Minneapolis: Abdo Publishing, 2023.

NOTE TO EDUCATORS

Visit **www.focusreaders.com** to find lesson plans, activities, links, and other resources related to this title.

INDEX

Blue Origin, 29–33

capsule, 5–6, 29–32

Dragon, 23–24, 40–41
Dream Chaser, 36–37

Falcon 9, 23–25, 26–27, 39, 45

ISS, 21, 33, 37, 39–40

NASA, 17, 19–21, 37, 39, 43
New Glenn, 32–33
New Shepard, 29–32

payloads, 15, 17, 25, 32–33, 39–40
propellants, 11, 13, 20, 24

satellites, 6, 15, 33, 39, 45
Sierra Nevada Corporation, 36

SpaceShipTwo, 35–36
space tourists, 5–6, 29–31, 36, 40
SpaceX, 23–25, 26, 29–30, 39–43, 44–45
Starship, 42–43
steering, 13, 25, 30, 32

Virgin Galactic, 35–36

X-33, 19–20

Answer Key: 1. Answers will vary; 2. Answers will vary; 3. B; 4. A